SHENANDOAH NATIONAL PARK ACTIVITY BOOK

PUZZLES, MAZES, GAMES, AND MORE ABOUT SHENANDOAH NATIONAL PARK

NATIONAL PARKS ACTIVITIES SERIES

SHENANDOAH NATIONAL PARK ACTIVITY BOOK

Copyright 2022
Published by Little Bison Press

The author acknowledges that the land on which Shenandoah National Park is located are the traditional lands the Manahoac Tribe.

For more free national parks activities, visit Littlebisonpress.com

About Shenandoah National Park

Shenandoah National Park is located in the state of Virginia. The park sits along the Blue Ridge Mountains and is home to deer, songbirds, black bears, as well as hundreds more plants and animal species.

This park is famous for its 500 miles of hiking, horseback riding, and biking trails, including 100 miles of the famous Appalachian Trail. The park is bursting with cascading waterfalls, breathtaking vistas, fields of wildflowers, and peaceful backwoods.

Visitors can stop by the historic Rapidan Camp, President Herbert Hoover's rustic and beautiful summer retreat. Rapidan Camp was built before Camp David, and it was here that the President would relax, away from his many responsibilities.

Shenandoah National Park is famous for:
- 500 miles of hiking, horseback riding, and biking trails
- sharp, jagged mountain peaks
- beautiful wildflowers
- quiet wooded hollows

Hey! I'm Parker!

I'm the only snail in history to visit every National Park in the United States! Come join me on my adventures in Shenandoah National Park.

Throughout this book, we will learn about the history of the park, the animals and plants that live here, and things to do here if you ever get to visit in person. This book is also full of games and activities!

Last but not least, I am hidden 9 times on different pages. See how many times you can find me. This page doesn't count!

Shenandoah Bingo

Let's play bingo! Cross off each box that you are able to during your visit to the national park. Try to get a bingo down, across, or diagonally. If you can't visit the park, use the bingo board to plan your perfect trip.

Pick out some activities that you would want to do during your visit. What would you do first? How long would you spend there? What animals would you try to see?

SPOT A SALAMANDER	SEE A ROCK OUTCROP	GO FOR A HIKE	TAKE A PICTURE AT AN OVERLOOK	WATCH A MOVIE AT THE VISITORS CENTER
IDENTIFY A TREE	LEARN ABOUT THE INDIGENOUS PEOPLE THAT LIVE IN THIS AREA	WITNESS A SUNRISE OR SUNSET	OBSERVE THE NIGHT SKIES	GO SNOWSHOEING
HEAR A BIRD CALL	SPOT A WATERFALL	FREE SPACE	LEARN ABOUT THE IMPORTANCE OF BROOK TROUT	SPOT SOME ANIMAL TRACKS
PICK UP TEN PIECES OF TRASH	HAVE A PICNIC	SEE A WHITE-TAILED DEER	VISIT SKYLAND	SPOT A BIRD OF PREY
LEARN ABOUT THE GEOLOGY OF BLUE RIDGE	SEE SOMEONE RIDING A HORSE	GO CAMPING	VISIT A RANGER STATION	PARTICIPATE IN A RANGER-LED ACTIVITY

Bird Scavenger Hunt

Shenandoah National Park is a great place to go birdwatching. You don't have to be able to identify different species of birds in order to have fun. Open your eyes and tune in your ears. Check off as many birds on this list as you can.

- [ ] A colorful bird
- [ ] A brown bird
- [ ] A bird in a tree
- [ ] A bird with long tail feathers
- [ ] A bird making noise
- [ ] A bird eating or hunting
- [ ] A bird with spots

- [ ] A big bird
- [ ] A small bird
- [ ] A hopping bird
- [ ] A flying bird
- [ ] A bird's nest
- [ ] A bird's footprint on the ground
- [ ] A bird with stripes somewhere on it

What was the easiest bird on the list to find? What was the hardest? Why do you think that was?

_____
_____
_____

Take a Hike

Go for a hike with your friends or family. If you aren't able to visit Shenandoah National Park, go for a walk in a park near where you live. Read through the prompts before your walk and finish the activities after you return.

Draw something you saw that moves:

Draw something you saw when you looked up:

Draw something you saw that grows out of the ground:

Draw a picture of your favorite part of the walk:

Rain, Rain, Rain

If it rains while you are visiting Shenandoah National Park, you can do this activity during your trip. If you don't get any rain while you are there, you can follow the same instructions next time it rains where you live.

Go outside into the rain. Use all of your senses as you complete the boxes below. You can use words, drawings, or both.

Sit as still as you can and listen to the rain. How does it make you feel?

Look straight up at the sky and let the raindrops fall on your face. Close your eyes. How does it feel?

Watch where the rain goes. Pay attention to the different surfaces the rain lands on. Which surfaces absorb the rain, and which surfaces cause the rain to run off or pool?

Are there any animals or bugs out enjoying the rain? Do you think the plants are enjoying the rain?

Go Horseback Riding on the Rose River Trail

Help find the horse's lost shoe!

DID YOU KNOW?

Horseback riding is a popular activity in Shenandoah National Park. There are many trails that you can take horses for day or overnight trips.

Camping Packing List

What should you take with you camping? Pretend you are in charge of your family camping trip. Make a list of what you would need to be safe and comfortable on an overnight excursion. Some considerations are listed on the side.

1.
2.
3.
4.
5.
6.
7.
8.
9.
10.
11.
12.
13.
14.
15.
16.

- What will you eat at every meal?
- What will the weather be like?
- Where will you sleep?
- What will you do during your free time?
- How luxurious do you want camp to be?
- How will you cook?
- How will you see at night?
- How will you dispose of trash?
- What might you need in case of emergencies?

9

Shenandoah National Park

Visitor's Log

Date:

Season:

Who I went with:

Which entrance:

How was your experience? Write a few sentences on your trip. Where did you stay? What did you do? What was your favorite activity? If you have not yet visited the park, write a paragraph pretending that you did.

_____
_____
_____
_____
_____
_____

STAMPS

Many national parks and monuments have cancellation stamps for visitors to use. These rubber stamps record the date and the location that you visited. Many people collect the markings as a free souvenir. Check with a ranger to see where you can find a stamp during your visit. If you aren't able to find one, you can draw your own.

Where is the Park?

Shenandoah National Park is in the eastern United States. It is located in Virginia, just 75 miles from Washington, D.C.!

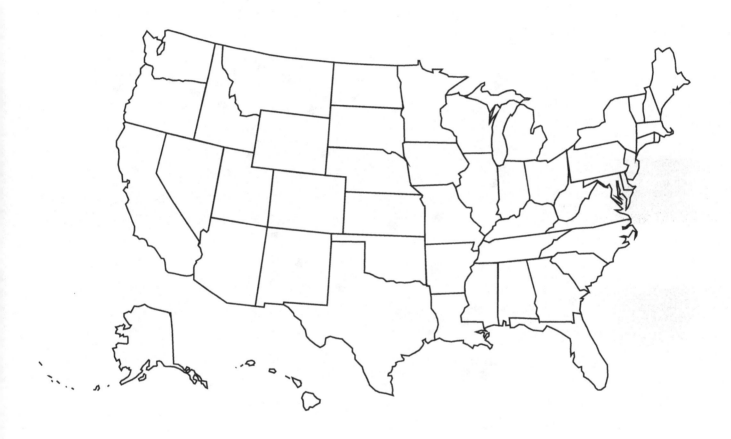

Virginia

Look at the shape of Virginia Can you find it on the map? If you are from the US, can you find your home state? Color Virginia red. Put a star on the map where you live.

Connect the Dots #1

Connect the dots to figure out what this tiny critter is. One species of this animal lives in Shenandoah National Park.

Their heart rate can reach as high as 1,260 beats per minute and a breathing rate of 250 breaths per minute. Have you ever measured your breathing rate? Ask a friend or family member to set a timer for 60 seconds. Once they say "go", try to breathe normally. Count each breath until they say "stop." How do your breaths per minute compare to hummingbirds?

_____

_____

The Kestrel is a colorful falcon and one of the smallest birds of prey in the US with a length of 9-12 inches. You might spot it hunting rodents in the meadows of Shenandoah NP.

Milk Snakes are not venomous. They are often confused with dangerous copperhead or coral snakes; however, they pose no threat to humans.

Who lives here?

Here are eight plants and animals that live in the park.
Use the word bank to fill in the clues below.

WORD BANK: BEAVER, CHICORY, MILK SNAKE, FISHER, GINSENG, KESTREL, BLUEGILL, OVENBIRD

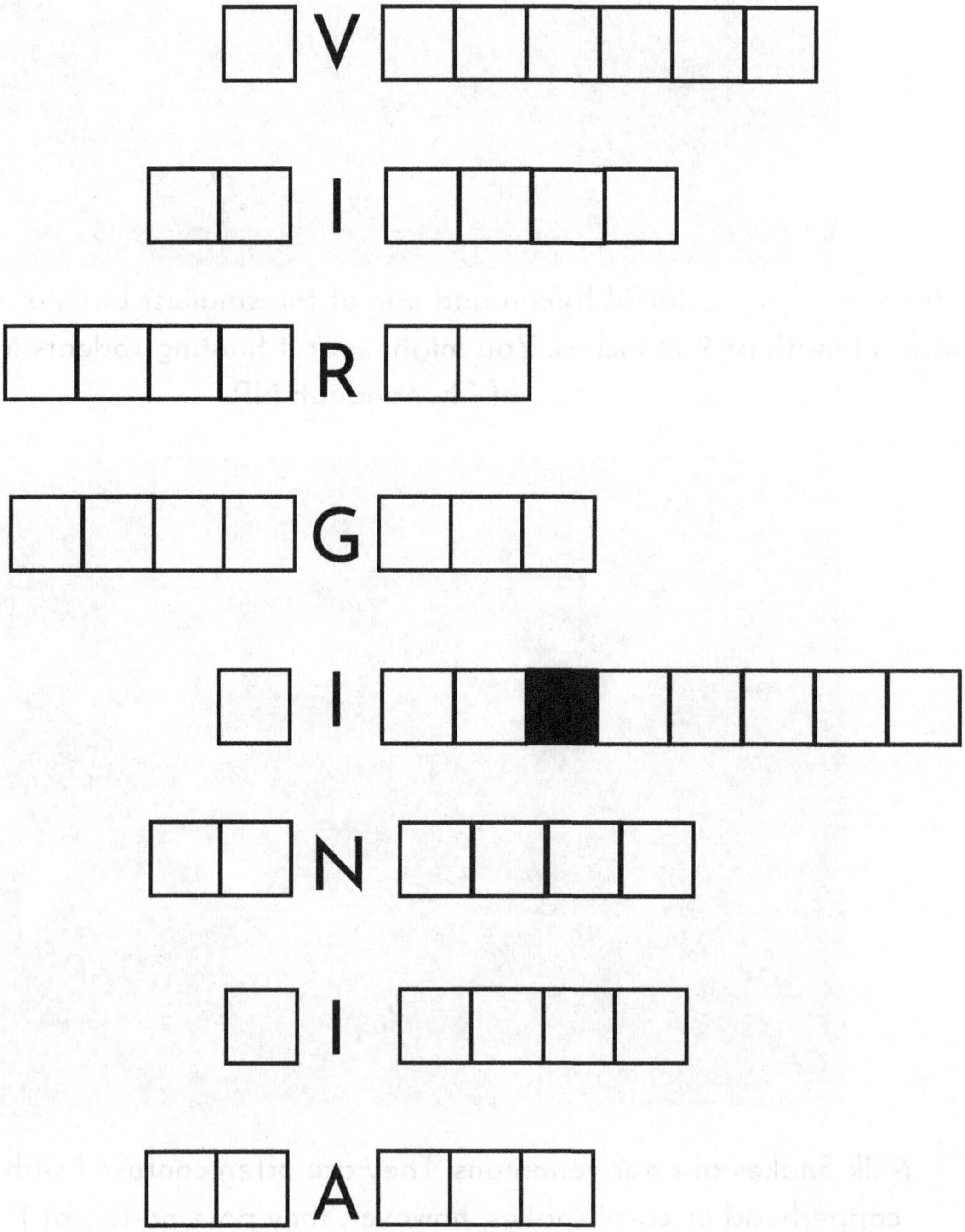

☐ V ☐ ☐ ☐ ☐ ☐

☐ ☐ I ☐ ☐ ☐

☐ ☐ ☐ R ☐ ☐

☐ ☐ ☐ G ☐ ☐

☐ I ☐ ☐ ■ ☐ ☐ ☐ ☐

☐ ☐ N ☐ ☐ ☐

☐ I ☐ ☐ ☐

☐ ☐ A ☐ ☐

Fishers are members of the weasel family. They make their dens in natural cavities, such as trees, logs, and rocky outcrops.

Beavers are the largest North American rodent.

Common Names
vs.
Scientific Names

A common name of an organism is a name that is based on everyday language. You have heard the common names of plants, animals, and other living things on tv, in books, and at school. Common names can also be referred to as "English" names, popular names, or farmer's name. Common names can vary from place to place. The word for a particular tree may be one thing, but that same tree has a different name in another country. Common names can even vary from region to region, even in the same country.

Scientific names, or Latin names, are given to organisms to make it possible to have uniform names for the same species. Scientific names are in Latin. You may have heard plants or animals referred to by their scientific name, or at least parts of their scientific names. Latin names are also called "binomial nomenclature" which refers to a two-part naming system. The first part of the name - the generic name - names the genus to which the species belongs. The second part of the name, the specific name, identifies the species. For example, Tyrannosaurus rex is an example of a widely known scientific name.

American Black Bear
Ursus americanus

COMMON NAME

Coyote
Canis latrans

LATIN NAME = GENUS + SPECIES

Coyote = Canis latrans

Black Bear = Ursus americanus

Find the Match!
Common Names and Latin Names

Match the common name to the scientific name for each animal. The first one is done for you. Use clues on the page before and after this one to complete the matches.

Bobcat	Haliaeetus leucocephalus
White Camass	Ursus americanus
White Oak ──┐	Pandion haliaetus
American Black Bear │	Ondatra zibethicus
Great Horned Owl │	Anticlea glauca
Bald Eagle │	Lampropeltis getula
Osprey │	Bubo virginianus
Muskrat │	Lynx rufus
Eastern Kingsnake └─	Quercus alba

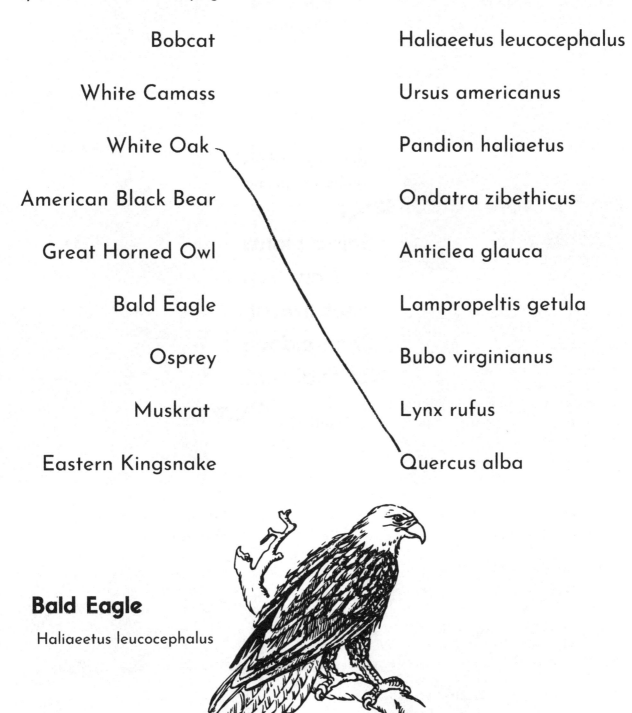

Bald Eagle
Haliaeetus leucocephalus

Osprey
Pandion Haliaetus

Bobcat
Lynx rufus

Great Horned Owl
Bubo virginianus

Some plants and animals that live at Shenandoah National Park

White Oak
Quercus alba

Muskrat
Ondatra Zibethicus

Eastern Kingsnake
Quercus alba

Things to Do Jumble

Unscramble the letters to uncover activities you can do while in Shenandoah National Park. Hint: each one ends in -ing.

1. NGSI ☐☐☐☐ING
2. KHI ☐☐☐ING
3. IRDB ☐☐☐☐ING
4. MACP ☐☐☐☐ING
5. KINICPC ☐☐☐☐☐☐☐ING
6. EISSTEHG ☐☐☐☐☐☐☐☐ING
7. SARTGZA ☐☐☐☐☐☐☐ING

Word Bank

birding
reading
camping
stargazing
horseback riding
hiking
hunting
singing
yelling
sightseeing
picnicking

19

Map Symbol Sudoku

The National Park System makes park maps using symbols instead of words. They are easily understood and take up way less space on a tiny map.

Trailhead   Waterfall   Wilderness   Campground

Complete this symbol sudoku puzzle. Fill each square with one of the symbols. Each one can appear only once in each row, column, and mini 2x2 grid. Each symbol means something, so you can write what the symbol represents instead of drawing the symbols if you prefer.

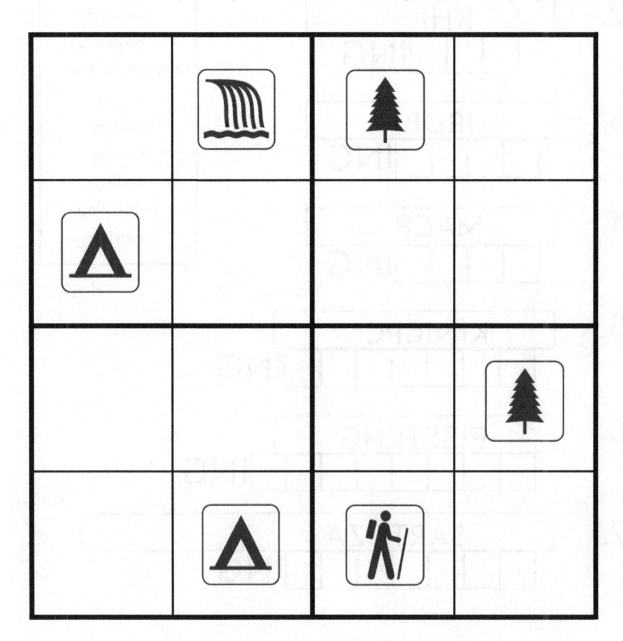

The National Park Logo

The National Park System has over 400 units in the US. Just like Shenandoah National Park, each location is unique or special in some way. The areas include other national parks, historic sites, monuments, seashores, and other recreation areas.

Each element of the National Park emblem represents something that the National Park Service protects. Fill in each blank below to show what each symbol represents.

WORD BANK:

MOUNTAINS, ARROWHEAD, BISON, SEQUOIA TREE, WATER

This represents all plants. _____

This represents all animals. _____

This symbol represents the landscapes. _____

This represents the waters protected by the park service. _____

This represents the historical and archeological values. _____

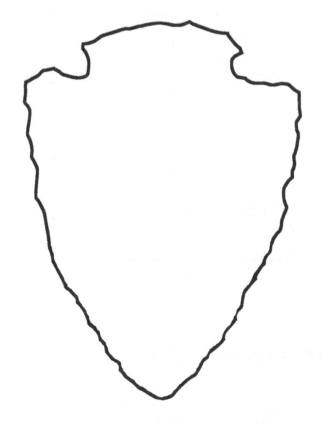

Now it's your turn! Pretend you are designing a new national park. Add elements to the design that represent the things that your park protects

What is the name of your park?

Describe why you included the symbols that you included. What do they mean?

The Ten Essentials

The ten essentials is a list of things that are important to have when you go for longer hikes. If you go on a hike to the <u>backcountry</u>, it is especially important that you have everything you need in case of an emergency. If you get lost or something unforeseen happens, it is good to be prepared to survive until help finds you.

The ten essentials list was developed in the 1930s by an outdoors group called the Mountaineers. Over time and technological advancements, this list has evolved. Can you identify all the things on the current list? Circle each of the "essentials" and cross out everything that doesn't make the cut.

fire: matches, lighter, tinder and/or stove	a pint of milk	extra money	headlamp plus extra batteries	extra clothes
extra water	a dog	Polaroid camera	bug net	lightweight games, like a deck of cards
extra food	a roll of duct tape	shelter	sun protection like sunglasses, sun-protective clothes and sunscreen	knife: plus a gear repair kit
a mirror	navigation: map, compass, altimeter, GPS device, or satellite messenger	first aid kit	extra flip-flops	entertainment like video games or books

Backcountry- a remote undeveloped rural area.

Connect the Dots #2

This animal lives in almost every state in the US, including the national park. They are nocturnal and are more active at night and sleep during the day. They are omnivorous eaters, which means they eat both plants and animals.

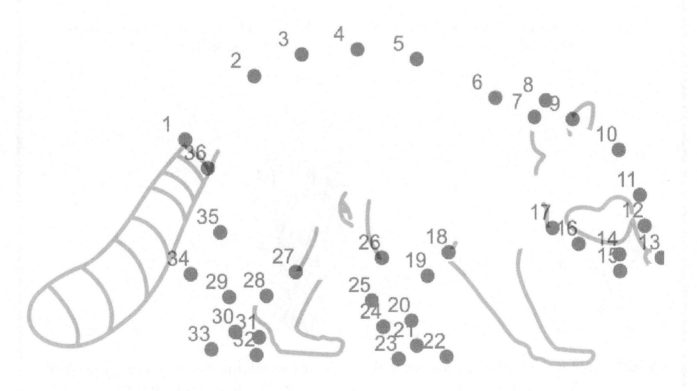

Are you an omnivore like a raccoon? An herbivore only eats plant foods. A carnivore only eats meat. An omnivore eats both. What type of eater are you? Write down some of your favorite foods to back up your answer.

_____
_____

Protecting the Park

When you visit national parks, it is important to leave the park the way you found it. Did you know that the national parks get hundreds of millions of visitors every year? We can only protect national parks for future visitors to enjoy if everyone does their part. The choices that each visitor makes when visiting the park have a big impact all together.

Read each line below. Write a sentence or draw a picture to show the impacts these changes would make on the park.

What would happen if every visitor fed the wild animals?

What would happen if every visitor picked a flower?

What would happen if every visitor took home a few rocks?

What would happen if every visitor wrote or carved their name on the rocks or trees?

Shenandoah Word Search

Words may be horizontal, vertical, or diagonal and they might be backward!

1. hills
2. virginia
3. deer
4. rare plants
5. rustic
6. cabins
7. hoover
8. fishing
9. wildlife
10. Skyline Drive
11. rocks
12. Appalachian
13. hiking
14. vacation
15. White oak
16. WPA
17. backpacking

```
C W F I S H I N G S K L O W K
H T A S H I L L S H E L A N J
R O C K S K O S C C L D E E R
A M P A A I N I G R I V U C U
R E A D I N B L O E I U J A S
E O L D T G O A D C T E A S T
P E S T W I L D L I F E I C I
L L B A M U I E G W V E K N C
A P W S G M L O B I A D Y A M
N C I H O O V E R I C K O I A
T T A H C H I D O O A E N H N
S R N I S O E I S O T K I C E
I I O S H N I R E I I A L A W
J C G O I O I T S O O R V L H
N I C L K M I B E R N L H A A
X T Y F A H E G A Z E S Q P L
H K D R W E L E C C R I C P E
S J D O G N I K C A P K C A B
```

25

Wildlife Wisdom

The national park is home to a lot of different kinds of animals. Seeing wildlife can be an exciting thing about visiting the national park but it is important to remember that these animals are wild. They need plenty of space and a healthy habitat where they can find their own food. Part of this is not allowing animals to eat any human food. This is their home and we are the visitors. We need to be respectful of the wildlife in the park.

Directions: Circle the highlighted words that best complete the following sentences.

If an animal changes its behavior because of your presence, you are:
   A) too close
   B) funny looking
   C) dehydrated and should drink more water

The best thing we can do to help wild animals survive is:
   A) make them pets
   B) protect their habitat
   C) knit them winter sweaters

In a national park, it is okay to share your food with wild animals:
   A) never
   B) always
   C) sometimes

When you're hiking in an area where there are bears, you should warn bears that you are entering their space by:
   A) hiking quietly
   B) making noise
   C) wearing bright colors

At night, park rangers care for the animals by:
   A) putting them back into their cages
   B) tucking them into bed
   C) leaving them alone

If you see an abandoned bird's nest, it is best to:
   A) pet the baby birds
   B) leave it alone
   C) crunch the empty eggshells

Bears look under logs in hopes of finding:
   A) granola bars
   B) insects
   C) peanuts to eat

The place where an animal lives is called its
   A) condo
   B) habitat
   C) crib

Color Skyline Drive

Skyline drive curves 105 miles through the park. There are almost 70 overlooks where you can stop for a glimpse at the view or to look for wildlife.

The Perfect Picnic Spot

Fill in the blanks on this page without looking at the full story. Once you have each line filled out, use the words you've chosen to complete the story on the next page.

EMOTION _____

FOOD _____

SOMETHING SWEET _____

STORE _____

MODE OF TRANSPORTATION _____

NOUN _____

SOMETHING ALIVE _____

SAUCE _____

PLURAL VEGETABLES _____

ADJECTIVE _____

PLURAL BODY PART _____

ANIMAL _____

PLURAL FRUIT _____

PLACE _____

SOMETHING TALL _____

COLOR _____

ADJECTIVE _____

NOUN _____

A DIFFERENT ANIMAL _____

FAMILY MEMBER #1 _____

FAMILY MEMBER #2 _____

VERB THAT ENDS IN -ING _____

A DIFFERENT FOOD _____

The Perfect Picnic Spot

Use the words from the previous page to complete a silly story.

When my family suggested having our lunch at the Big Meadows picnic area, I

was _____. I love eating my _____ outside! I knew we had picked up a
     EMOTION   FOOD

box of _____ from the _____ for after lunch, my favorite. We drove up
    SOMETHING SWEET   STORE

to the area and I jumped out of the _____. "I will find the perfect spot for
                                         MODE OF TRANSPORTATION

a picnic!" I grabbed a _____ for us to sit on, and I ran off. I passed a picnic
                       NOUN

table, but it was covered with _____ so we couldn't sit there. The next
                              SOMETHING ALIVE

picnic table looked okay, but there were smears of _____ and pieces of
                                                    SAUCE

_____ everywhere. The people that were there before must have been
PLURAL VEGETABLES

_____! I gritted my _____ together and kept walking down the path,
ADJECTIVE   PLURAL BODY PART

determined to find the perfect spot. I wanted a table with a good view of the

trees. Why was this so hard? If we were lucky, I might even get to see _____
                                                                        ANIMAL

eating some _____ on the hillside. They don't have those in _____ where I
          PLURAL FRUIT   PLACE

am from. I walked down a little hill and there it was, the perfect spot! The trees

towered overhead and looked as tall as _____. The patch of grass was a
                                            SOMETHING TALL

beautiful _____ color. The _____ flowers were growing on
        COLOR   ADJECTIVE

the side of a _____. I looked across the meadow and even saw a
           NOUN

_____ on the edge of a rock. I looked back to see my _____ and
DIFFERENT ANIMAL   FAMILY MEMBER #1

_____ _____ a picnic basket. "I hope you brought plenty of
FAMILY MEMBER #2 VERB THAT ENDS IN ING

_____, I'm starving!"
A DIFFERENT FOOD

29

Hike to a Waterfall

start here →

DID YOU KNOW? There are dozens of waterfalls in Shenandoah NP and dozens more in the Blue Ridge Mountains.

Rapidan Camp Theme Word Search

Visitors to Shenandoah National Park can visit Rapidan Camp, President Herbert Hoover's rustic and beautiful summer retreat.

1. Hoover
2. rustic
3. retreat
4. brown house
5. president
6. fishing
7. cabin
8. fireplace
9. schoolhouse
10. opossum
11. marine
12. cabinet
13. trout
14. Mill Prong
15. hike
16. historic
17. copper

```
L D E S S U O P H I D E O W C
H A D A M P A Z S W E R W T P
T V H O O V E R A W A L K E R
S E U S S P T U O R T T B N E
C N S A E Q Y S L E Y R S I S
M U D L Y R R T A E R E R B I
M A R I N E C I R H L R L A D
A R B E M K I C D I L S V C E
L T H F I S H I N G U D E P N
L O I C I M O Y K E U G R T T
I S A I B R O W N H O U S E N
S H R R K A E I S A S K T R E
T J E O F H I P Z I H I K E C
E Y P T L I V E L N D R V E O
R W P S D O R A D A A O H E M
T T O I G R E E N L C A B I N
U S C H O O L H O U S E V E B
C J D M I L L P R O N G I O N
```

31

Leave No Trace Quiz

Leave No Trace is a concept that helps people make decisions during outdoor recreation that protects the environment. There are seven principles that guide us when we spend time outdoors, whether you are in a national park or not. Are you an expert in Leave No Trace? Take this quiz and find out!

1. How can you plan ahead and prepare to ensure you have the best experience you can in the national park?
    a. Make sure you stop by the ranger station for a map and to ask about current conditions.
    b. Just wing it! You will know the best trail when you see it.
    c. Stick to your plan, even if conditions change. You traveled a long way to get here, and you should stick to your plan.
2. What is an example of traveling on a durable surface?
    a. Walking only on the designated path.
    b. Walking on the grass that borders the trail if the trail is very muddy.
    c. Taking a shortcut if you can find one since it means you will be walking less.
3. Why should you dispose of waste properly?
    a. You don't need to. Park rangers love to pick up the trash you leave behind.
    b. You actually should leave your leftovers behind, because animals will eat them. It is important to make sure they aren't hungry.
    c. So that other peoples' experiences of the park are not impacted by you leaving your waste behind.
4. How can you best follow the concept "leave what you find"?
    a. Take only a small rock or leaf to remember your trip.
    b. Take pictures, but leave any physical items where they are.
    c. Leave everything you find, unless it may be rare like an arrowhead, then it is okay to take.
5. What is not a good example of minimizing campfire impacts?
    a. Only having a campfire in a pre-existing campfire ring.
    b. Checking in with current conditions when you consider making a campfire.
    c. Building a new campfire ring in a location that has a better view.
6. What is a poor example of respecting wildlife?
    a. Building squirrel houses out of rocks so the squirrels have a place to live.
    b. Stay far away from wildlife and give them plenty of space.
    c. Reminding your grown-ups to not drive too fast in animal habitats while visiting the park.
7. How can you show consideration of other visitors?
    a. Play music on your speaker so other people at the campground can enjoy it.
    b. Wear headphones on the trail if you choose to listen to music.
    c. Make sure to yell "Hello!" to every animal you see at top volume.

Park Poetry

America's parks inspire art of all kinds. Painters, sculptors, photographers, writers, and artists of all mediums have taken inspiration from natural beauty. They have turned their inspiration into great works.

Use this space to write your own poem about the park. Think about what you have experienced or seen. Use descriptive language to create an acrostic poem. This type of poem has the first letter of each line spell out another word. Create an acrostic that spells out the word "Forest."

F _____

O _____

R _____

E _____

S _____

T _____

Fresh air
Open skies
Ready to
Explore
So many
Towering trees

Family time
On our way
Relaxing
Everyone excited
Singing songs
Terrifc memories

Making a Difference

It is important to protect the valuable resources of the world, not just beautiful places like national parks.

How many of these things do you do at home? If you answered "no" to more than 10 items, talk to the grownups in your life to see if there are any household habits you might be able to change. Conserving our collective resources helps us all.

Yes	No	Do you...
☐	☐	turn off the water when you are brushing your teeth?
☐	☐	use LED light bulbs when possible?
☐	☐	use a reusable water bottle instead of disposable ones?
☐	☐	ride your bike or take the bus instead of riding in the car?
☐	☐	have a rain barrel under your roof gutters to collect rain water?
☐	☐	take quick showers?
☐	☐	avoid putting more food on your plate than you will eat?
☐	☐	take reusable lunch containers?
☐	☐	grow a garden?
☐	☐	buy items with less packaging?
☐	☐	recycle paper?
☐	☐	recycle plastic?
☐	☐	have a compost pile at home so you can make your own soil?
☐	☐	pick up trash when you see it on the trail?
☐	☐	plan a "staycation" and fly only when you have to?

_____ _____
 # of   # of
 Yes   No

Add up your score! Are there any "no"s that you want to turn into a yes?

Can you think of any other ways to protect our natural resources?

_____

Catch a Fish in the Rapidan River

start here

Grab a fishing pole and try to reel in a fish.

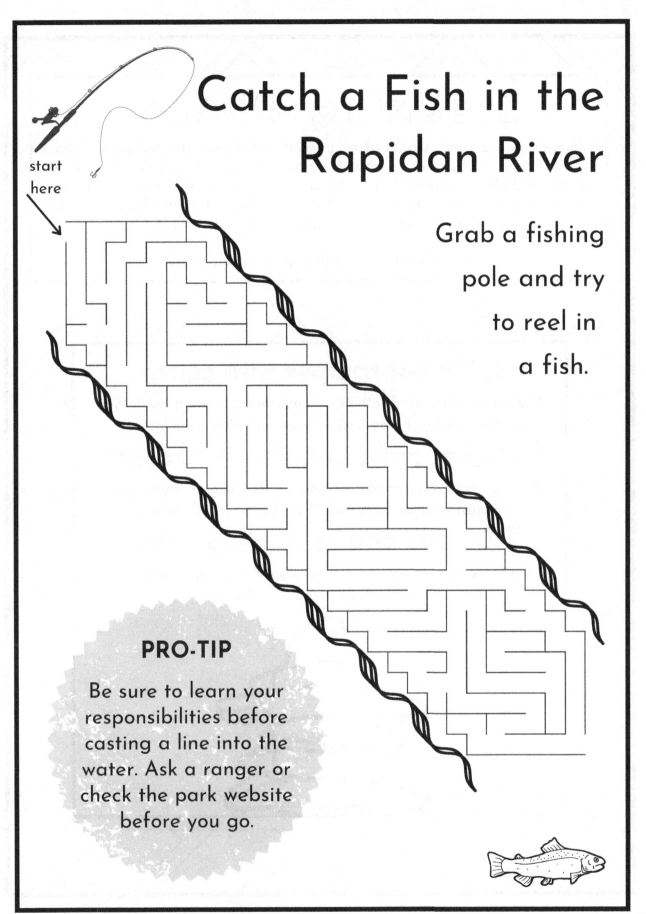

PRO-TIP

Be sure to learn your responsibilities before casting a line into the water. Ask a ranger or check the park website before you go.

Stacking Rocks

Have you ever seen stacks of rocks while hiking in national parks? Do you know what they are or what they mean? These rock piles are called cairns and often mark hiking routes in parks. Every park has a different way to maintain trails and cairns. However, they all have the same rule: If you come across a cairn, do not disturb it.

Color the cairn and the rules to remember.

1. Do not tamper with cairns.

If a cairn is tampered with or an unauthorized one is built, then future visitors may become disoriented or even lost.

2. Do not build unauthorized cairns.

Moving rocks disturbs the soil and makes the area more prone to erosion. Disturbing rocks can disturb fragile plants.

3. Do not add to existing cairns.

Authorized cairns are carefully designed. Adding to them can actually cause them to collapse.

Decoding Using American Sign Language

American Sign Language, also called ASL for short, is a language that many Deaf people or people who are hard of hearing use to communicate. People use ASL to communicate with their hands. Did you know people from all over the country and world travel to national parks? You may hear people speaking other languages. You might also see people using ASL. Use the American Manual Alphabet chart to decode some national parks facts.

This was the first national park to be established:

This is the biggest national park in the US:

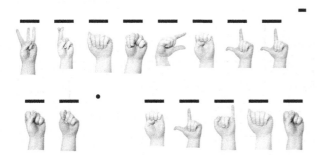

This is the most visited national park:

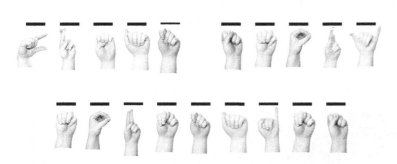

Hint: Pay close attention to the position of the thumb!

 Try it! Using the chart, try to make the letters of the alphabet with your hand. What is the hardest letter to make? Can you spell out your name? Show a friend or family member and have them watch you spell out the name of the national park you are in.

Go Birdwatching at Fox Hollow Trail

DID YOU KNOW? Shenandoah National Park is home to several birds of prey, including eagles, hawks, and owls. Birds of prey are birds that hunt other animals for food.

Butterflies of Shenandoah NP

Dozens of species of butterflies and moths live in Shenandoah National Park. Their wingspan size varies, as do the patterns on their wings. Design your butterfly below. Make sure the wings are symmetrical, meaning both sides match.

A Hike to Blackrock

Fill in the blanks on this page without looking at the full story. Once you have each line filled out, use the words you've chosen to complete the story on the next page.

ADJECTIVE _____

SOMETHING TO EAT _____

SOMETHING TO DRINK _____

NOUN _____

ARTICLE OF CLOTHING _____

BODY PART _____

VERB _____

ANIMAL _____

SAME TYPE OF FOOD _____

ADJECTIVE _____

SAME ANIMAL _____

VERB THAT ENDS IN "ED" _____

NUMBER _____

A DIFFERENT NUMBER _____

SOMETHING THAT FLIES _____

LIGHT SOURCE _____

PLURAL NOUN _____

FAMILY MEMBER _____

YOUR NICKNAME _____

A Hike to Blackrock

Use the words from the previous page to complete a silly story.

I went for a hike to Blackrock today. In my favorite _____ backpack, I
                                                      ADJECTIVE

made sure to pack a map so I wouldn't get lost. I also threw in an extra

_____ just in case I got hungry and a bottle of _____. I put
SOMETHING TO EAT   SOMETHING TO DRINK

on my _____ spray, and a tied a _____ around my
       NOUN   ARTICLE OF CLOTHING

_____, in case it gets chilly. I started to _____ down the path. As
BODY PART   VERB

soon as I turned the corner, I came face to face with a(n) _____. I think
                                                           ANIMAL

it was as startled as I was! What should I do? I had to think fast! Should I

give it some of my _____? No. I had to remember what the
                   SAME TYPE OF FOOD

_____ ranger told me. "If you see one, back away slowly and try not to
ADJECTIVE

scare it." Soon enough, the _____ _____ away. The coast
                            SAME ANIMAL   VERB THAT ENDS IN ED

was clear. _____ hours later, I finally got to the lookout. I felt like I could
            NUMBER

see for a _____ miles. I took a picture of a _____ so I could always
          A DIFFERENT NUMBER   NOUN

remember this moment. As I was putting my camera away, a _____
                                                          SOMETHING THAT FLIES

flew by, reminding me that it was almost nighttime. I turned on my

_____ and headed back. I could hear the _____ singing their
LIGHT SOURCE   PLURAL INSECT

evening song. Just as I was getting tired, I saw my _____ and our tent.
                                                    FAMILY MEMBER

        "Welcome back _____! How was your hike?"
                      NICKNAME

Reflections on Special Places

National parks are special places for all sorts of reasons. Can you think of an outdoor area that is special to you? It can be a place you love because your family is from there, or because it is beautiful, or because you can do your favorite things there.

What is a place (does not have to be a national park) that is special to you?

_____
_____
_____
_____

What do national parks mean to you?

_____
_____
_____

What is your favorite part of being able to enjoy the national parks around you?

_____
_____
_____
_____

Let's Go Camping Word Search

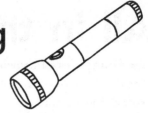

Words may be horizontal, vertical, or diagonal and they might be backward!

1. tent
2. camp stove
3. sleeping bag
4. bug spray
5. sunscreen
6. map
7. flashlight
8. pillow
9. lantern
10. ice
11. snacks
12. smores
13. water
14. first aid kit
15. chair
16. cards
17. books
18. games
19. trail
20. hat

```
D P P I L L O W D B T E A C I
E O A D P R E A A M B R C A N
P W C A M P S T O V E I H X G
R A H S G E L E B E E D A P S
E L B U G S P R A Y N G I E A
S I A H G C I C N N M E R C N
C W N L A F I R S K O O B F K
M T A E M I L E L H M R W L J
T A P R E A O R E S L B A A B
S M P A S R R T E N T L U S C
C E A I I R C G P E I U J H A
S S N A C K S S I M O K I L R
I J R S F O I S N J R A Q I D
C Y E T L E V E G U O R V G S
E W T A K C A B B S S O H H M
X J N F I R S T A I D K I T T
U A A E S S E N G E T P V A B
C J L I A R T D N A M A H A S
```

All in the Day of a Park Ranger

Park Rangers are hardworking individuals dedicated to protecting our parks, monuments, museums, and more. They take care of the natural and cultural resources for future generations. Rangers also help protect the visitors of the park. Their responsibilities are broad and they work both with the public and behind the scenes.

What have you seen park rangers do? Use your knowledge of the duties of park rangers to fill out a typical daily schedule, one activity for each hour. Feel free to make up your own, but some examples of activities are provided on the right. Read carefully, not all of the example activities are befitting a ranger!

Time	Activity
6 am	Lead a sunrise hike
7 am	
8 am	
9 am	
10 am	
11 am	
12 pm	Enjoy a lunch break outside
1 pm	
2 pm	
3 pm	
4 pm	Teach visitors about the geology of the mountain
5 pm	
6 pm	
7 pm	
8 pm	
9 pm	

- feed the bald eagles
- build trails for visitors to enjoy
- throw rocks off the side of the mountain
- rescue lost hikers
- study animal behavior
- record air quality data
- answer questions at the visitor center
- pick wildflowers
- pick up litter
- share marshmallows with squirrels
- repair handrails
- lead a class on a field trip
- catch frogs and make them race
- lead people on educational hikes
- write articles for the park website
- protect the river from pollution
- remove non-native plants from the park
- study how climate change is affecting the park
- give a talk about mountain lions
- lead a program for campers on kestrels

If you were a park ranger, which of the above tasks would you enjoy most?

_____

_____

Draw Yourself as a Park Ranger

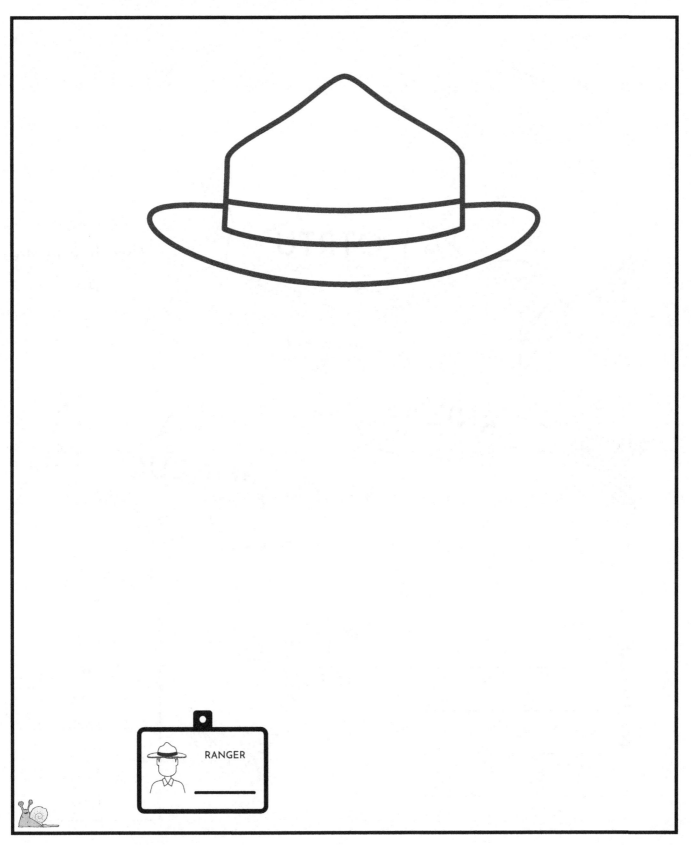

Fish at Shenandoah NP

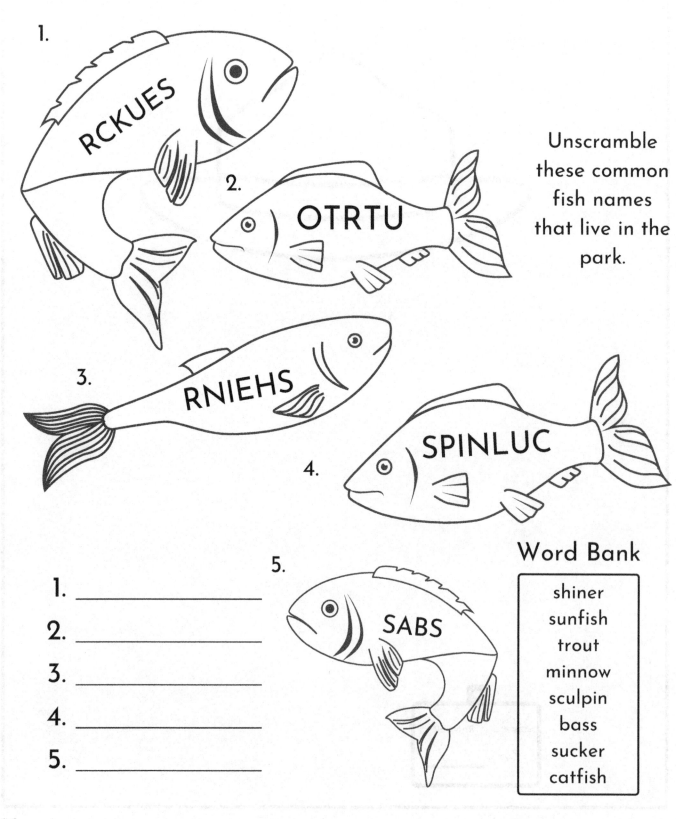

Unscramble these common fish names that live in the park.

1. RCKUES
2. OTRTU
3. RNIEHS
4. SPINLUC
5. SABS

1. _____
2. _____
3. _____
4. _____
5. _____

Word Bank

shiner
sunfish
trout
minnow
sculpin
bass
sucker
catfish

Amphibians

Two species of toads and eight species of frogs live in Shenandoah Park. Even more types of salamanders live there too. Frogs and toads both spend the beginning of their lives the same way, as tadpoles. Tadpoles hatch from eggs in water, usually in springs or pools of water.

Both frogs and toads are amphibians. Salamanders are amphibians too. Color the amphibians below.

 # Sound Exploration

Spend a minute or two listening to all of the sounds around you.
Draw your favorite sound.

How did this sound make you feel?
_____
_____

What did you think when you heard this sound?
_____
_____

Design a Water Bottle

Imagine you've been hired to design a reusable water bottle that will be for sale in the national park gift shop. It will be a souvenir for visitors to remember their trip to the park.

Consider adding a plant or animal that lives here, or include a famous place in the park or activity that you can do while visiting.

63 National Parks

How many other national parks have you been to? Which one do you want to visit next? Note that some of these parks fall on the border of more than one state, you may check it off more than once!

Alaska
☐ Denali National Park
☐ Gates of the Arctic National Park
☐ Glacier Bay National Park
☐ Katmai National Park
☐ Kenai Fjords National Park
☐ Kobuk Valley National Park
☐ Lake Clark National Park
☐ Wrangell-St. Elias National Park

American Samoa
☐ National Park of American Samoa

Arizona
☐ Grand Canyon National Park
☐ Petrified Forest National Park
☐ Saguaro National Park

Arkansas
☐ Hot Springs National Park

California
☐ Channel Islands National Park
☐ Death Valley National Park
☐ Joshua Tree National Park
☐ Kings Canyon National Park
☐ Lassen Volcanic National Park
☐ Pinnacles National Park
☐ Redwood National Park
☐ Sequoia National Park
☐ Yosemite National Park

Colorado
☐ Black Canyon of the Gunnison National Park
☐ Great Sand Dunes National Park
☐ Mesa Verde National Park
☐ Rocky Mountain National Park

Florida
☐ Biscayne National Park
☐ Dry Tortugas National Park
☐ Everglades National Park

Hawaii
☐ Haleakalā National Park
☐ Hawai'i Volcanoes National Park

Idaho
☐ Yellowstone National Park

Kentucky
☐ Mammoth Cave National Park

Indiana
☐ Indiana Dunes National Park

Maine
☐ Acadia National Park

Michigan
☐ Isle Royale National Park

Minnesota
☐ Voyageurs National Park

Missouri
☐ Gateway Arch National Park

Montana
☐ Glacier National Park
☐ Yellowstone National Park

Nevada
☐ Death Valley National Park
☐ Great Basin National Park

New Mexico
☐ Carlsbad Caverns National Park
☐ White Sands National Park

North Dakota
☐ Theodore Roosevelt National Park

North Carolina
☐ Great Smoky Mountains National Park

Ohio
☐ Cuyahoga Valley National Park

Oregon
☐ Crater Lake National Park

South Carolina
☐ Congaree National Park

South Dakota
☐ Badlands National Park
☐ Wind Cave National Park

Tennessee
☐ Great Smoky Mountains National Park

Texas
☐ Big Bend National Park
☐ Guadalupe Mountains National Park

Utah
☐ Arches National Park
☐ Bryce Canyon National Park
☐ Canyonlands National Park
☐ Capitol Reef National Park
☐ Zion National Park

Virgin Islands
☐ Virgin Islands National Park

Virginia
☐ Shenandoah National Park

Washington
☐ Mount Rainier National Park
☐ North Cascades National Park
☐ Olympic National Park

West Virginia
☐ New River Gorge National Park

Wyoming
☐ Grand Teton National Park
☐ Yellowstone National Park

Other National Parks

Besides Shenandoah National Park, there are 62 other diverse and beautiful national parks across the United States. Try your hand at this crossword. If you need help, look at the previous page for some hints.

Down

1. State where Acadia National Park is located
2. This national park has the Spanish word for turtle in it.
3. Number of national parks in Alaska
5. This national park has some of the hottest temperatures in the world.
6. This national park is the only one in Idaho.
7. This toothsome creature can be famously found in Everglades National Park.
8. Only president with a national park named for them

Across

4. This state has the most national parks.
9. This park has some of the newest land in the US, caused by volcanic eruptions.
10. This park has the deepest lake in the United States.
11. This color shows up in the name of a national park in California.
12. This national park deserves a gold medal.

Which National Park Will You Go to Next? Word Search

1. Zion
2. Big Bend
3. Glacier
4. Olympic
5. Sequoia
6. Bryce
7. Mesa Verde
8. Biscayne
9. Wind Cave
10. Great Basin
11. Katmai
12. Yellowstone
13. Voyageurs
14. Arches
15. Badlands
16. Denali
17. Glacier Bay
18. Hot Springs

```
F M M E S A V E R D E B N E Y
E A B I G B E N D E S A S E M
Y L I C A L O Y N E E D L T G
D M G A S S A U C N R L U E R
C E L I I T S C R E O A A K E
S N A W Y E E O I W T N A C A
G I C H A A Q C S E M D N S T
N O I Z P R U T I M R S N E B
I W E L M P O N B W E B K H A
R J R F D N I F L I H B U C S
P A B E E S A N E S O P W R I
S J A E N Y A C S I B A U A N
T C Y I A D O H H Y M E A L R
O T A T L M L E S E G R W R J
H S T O I K A T M A I R O P B
I C H U R C O L Y M P I C O U
O Y G T S D E O S B R Y C E T
W I N D C A V E I N R O H E M
```

Field Notes

Spend some time to reflect on your trip to Shenandoah National Park. Your field notes will help you remember the things you experienced. Use the space below to write about your day.

While I was at Shenandoah National Park...

I saw:
_____
_____
_____
_____
_____

I heard:
_____
_____
_____
_____

I felt:
_____
_____
_____

I wondered:
_____
_____
_____
_____

Draw a picture of your favorite thing in the park.

ANSWER KEY

Go Horseback Riding on the Rose River Trail

Help find the horse's lost shoe!

start here →

DID YOU KNOW?
Horseback riding is a popular activity in Shenandoah National Park. There are many trails that you can take horses for day or overnight trips.

Answers: Who lives here?

Here are eight plants and animals that live in the park.
Use the word bank to fill in the clues below.

WORD BANK: CHICORY, MILK SNAKE, FISHER, GINSENG, KESTREL, BLUEGILL, OVENBIRD, BEAVER

O **V** ENBIRD

CH **I** CORY

KEST **R** EL

BLUE **G** ILL

M **I** LK SNAKE

GI **N** SENG

F **I** SHER

BE **A** VER

Find the Match! Common Names and Latin Names

Match the common name to the scientific name for each animal. The first one is done for you. Use clues on the page before and after this one to complete the matches.

- Bobcat — Lynx rufus
- White Camass — Anticlea glauca
- White Oak — Quercus alba
- American Black Bear — Ursus americanus
- Great Horned Owl — Bubo virginianus
- Bald Eagle — Haliaeetus leucocephalus
- Osprey — Pandion haliaetus
- Muskrat — Ondatra zibethicus
- Eastern Kingsnake — Lampropeltis getula

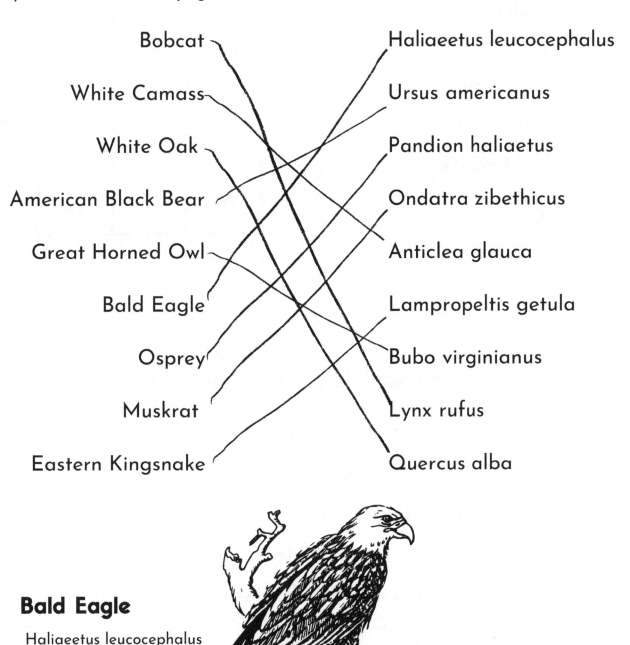

Bald Eagle

Haliaeetus leucocephalus

Jumbles Answers

1. SINGING
2. HIKING
3. BIRDING
4. CAMPING
5. PICNICKING
6. SIGHTSEEING
7. STAR GAZING

Map Symbol Sudoku Anwers

National Park Emblem Answers

1. This represents all plants. **Sequoia Tree**
2. This represents all animals. **Bison**
3. This symbol represents the landscapes. **Mountains**
4. This represents the waters protected by the park service. **Water**
5. This represents the historical and archeological values. **Arrowhead**

Answers: The Ten Essentials

The ten essentials is a list of things that are important to have when you go for longer hikes. If you go on a hike to the <u>backcountry</u>, it is especially important that you have everything you need in case of an emergency. If you get lost or something unforeseen happens, it is good to be prepared to survive until help finds you.

The ten essentials list was developed in the 1930s by an outdoors group called the Mountaineers. Over time and technological advancements, this list has evolved. Can you identify all the things on the current list? Circle each of the "essentials" and cross out everything that doesn't make the cut.

Backcountry- a remote undeveloped rural area.

59

Shenandoah Word Search

Words may be horizontal, vertical, or diagonal and they might be backward!

1. hills
2. virginia
3. deer
4. rare plants
5. rustic
6. cabins
7. hoover
8. fishing
9. wildlife
10. skyline drive
11. rocks
12. appalachian
13. hiking
14. vacation
15. white oak
16. wpa
17. backpacking

```
C W F I S H I N G S K L O W K
H T A S H I L L S H E L A N J
R O C K S K O S C C L D E E R
A M P A A I N I G R I V U C U
R E A D I N B L O E I U J A S
E O L D T G O A D C T E A S T
P E S T W I L D L I F E I C I
L L B A M U I E G W V E K N C
A P W S G M L O B I A D Y A M
N C I H O O V E R I C K O I A
T T A H C H I D O O A E N H N
S R N I S O E I S O T K I C E
  I I O S H N I R E I I A L A W
  J C G O I O I T S O O R V L H
  N I C L K M I B E R N L H A A
  X T Y F A H E G A Z E S Q P L
  H K D R W E L E C C R I C P E
  S J D O G N I K C A P K C A B
```

60

Wildlife Wisdom

The national park is home to a lot of different kinds of animals. Seeing wildlife can be an exciting thing about visiting the national park but it is important to remember that these animals are wild. They need plenty of space and a healthy habitat where they can find their own food. Part of this is not allowing animals to eat any human food. This is their home and we are the visitors. We need to be respectful of the wildlife in the park.

Directions: Circle the highlighted words that best complete the following sentences.

If an animal changes its behavior because of your presence, you are:
A) too close
B) funny looking
C) dehydrated and should drink more water

The best thing we can do to help wild animals survive is:
A) make them pets
B) protect their habitat
C) knit them winter sweaters

In a national park, it is okay to share your food with wild animals:
A) never
B) always
C) sometimes

When you're hiking in an area where there are bears, you should warn bears that you are entering their space by:
A) hiking quietly
B) making noise
C) wearing bright colors

At night, park rangers care for the animals by:
A) putting them back into their cages
B) tucking them into bed
C) leaving them alone

If you see an abandoned bird's nest, it is best to:
A) pet the baby birds
B) leave it alone
C) crunch the empty eggshells

Bears look under logs in hopes of finding:
A) granola bars
B) insects
C) peanuts to eat

The place where an animal lives is called its
A) condo
B) habitat
C) crib

Solution: Hike to a Waterfall

DID YOU KNOW? There are dozens of waterfalls in Shenandoah NP, and dozens more in the Blue Ridge Mountains.

Rapidan Camp Theme Word Search

Visitors to Shenandoah National Park can visit Rapidan Camp, President Herbert Hoover's rustic and beautiful summer retreat. It was recently restored to its 1929 appearance and is an excellent reflection of its era.

1. Hoover
2. rustic
3. retreat
4. brown house
5. president
6. fishing
7. cabin
8. fireplace
9. schoolhouse
10. opossum
11. marine
12. cabinet
13. trout
14. Mill Prong
15. hike
16. historic
17. copper

```
L D E S S U O P H I D E O W C
H A D A M P A Z S W E R W T P
T V H O O V E R A W A L K E R
S E U S S P T U O R T T B N E
C N S A E Q Y S L E Y R S I S
M U D L Y R R T A E R E R B I
M A R I N E C I R H L R L A D
A R B E M K I C D I L S V C E
L T H F I S H I N G U D E P N
L O I C I M O Y K E U G R T T
I S A I B R O W N H O U S E N
S H R R K A E I S A S K T R E
T J E O F H I P Z I H I K E C
E Y P T L I V E L N D R V E O
R W P S D O R A D A A O H E M
T T O I G R E E N L C A B I N
U S C H O O L H O U S E V E B
C J D M I L L P R O N G I O N
```

63

Answers: Leave No Trace Quiz

Leave No Trace is a concept that helps people make decisions during outdoor recreation that protects the environment. There are seven principles that guide us when we spend time outdoors, whether you are in a national park or not. Are you an expert in Leave No Trace? Take this quiz and find out!

1. How can you plan ahead and prepare to ensure you have the best experience you can in the National Park?
    A. Make sure you stop by the ranger station for a map and to ask about current conditions.
2. What is an example of traveling on a durable surface?
    A. Walking only on the designated path.
3. Why should you dispose of waste properly?
    C. So that other peoples' experiences of the park are not impacted by you leaving your waste behind.
4. How can you best follow the concept "leave what you find"?
    B. Take pictures but leave any physical items where they are.
5. What is not a good example of minimizing campfire impacts?
    C. Building a new campfire ring in a location that has a better view.
6. What is a poor example of respecting wildlife?
    A. Building squirrel houses out of rocks from the river so the squirrels have a place to live.
7. How can you show consideration of other visitors?
    B. Wear headphones on the trail if you choose to listen to music.

Solution: Catch a Fish in the Rapidan River

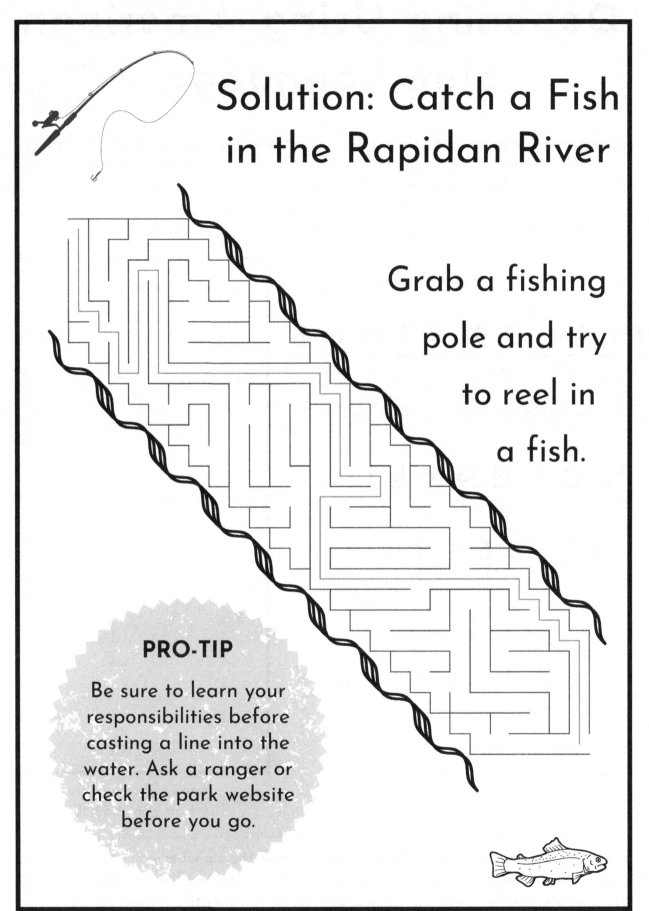

Grab a fishing pole and try to reel in a fish.

PRO-TIP

Be sure to learn your responsibilities before casting a line into the water. Ask a ranger or check the park website before you go.

Decoding Using American Sign Language

American Sign Language, also called ASL for short, is a language that many Deaf people or people who are hard of hearing use to communicate. People use ASL to communicate with their hands. Did you know people from all over the country and world travel to national parks? You may hear people speaking other languages. You might also see people using ASL. Use the American Manual Alphabet chart to decode some national parks facts.

This was the first national park to be established:

YELLOWSTONE

This is the biggest national park in the US:

WRANGELL-
ST. ELIAS

This is the most visited national park:

GREAT SMOKY
MOUNTAINS

Hint: Pay close attention to the position of the thumb!

Try it! Using the chart, try to make the letters of the alphabet with your hand. What is the hardest letter to make? Can you spell out your name? Show a friend or family member and have them watch you spell out the name of the national park you are in.

66

Go Birdwatching at Fox Hollow Trail

start here

DID YOU KNOW? Shenandoah NP is home to several birds of prey, including eagles, hawks, and owls. Birds of prey are birds that hunt other animals for food.

Let's Go Camping Word Search

1. tent
2. camp stove
3. sleeping bag
4. bug spray
5. sunscreen
6. map
7. flashlight
8. pillow
9. lantern
10. ice
11. snacks
12. smores
13. water
14. first aid kit
15. chair
16. cards
17. books
18. games
19. trail
20. hat

```
D P P I L L O W D B T E A C I
E O A D P R E A A M B R C A N
P W C A M P S T O V E I H X G
R A H S G E L E B E E D A P S
E L B U G S P R A Y N G I E A
S I A H G C I C N N M E R C N
C W N L A F I R S K O O B F K
M T A E M I L E L H M R W L J
T A P R E A O R E S L B A A B
S M P A S R R T E N T L U S C
C E A I I R C G P E I U J H A
S S N A C K S S I M O K I L R
I J R S F O I S N J R A Q I D
C Y E T L E V E G U O R V G S
E W T A K C A B B S S O H H M
X J N F I R S T A I D K I T T
U A A E S S E N G E T P V A B
C J L I A R T D N A M A H A S
```

Fish at Shenandoah NP

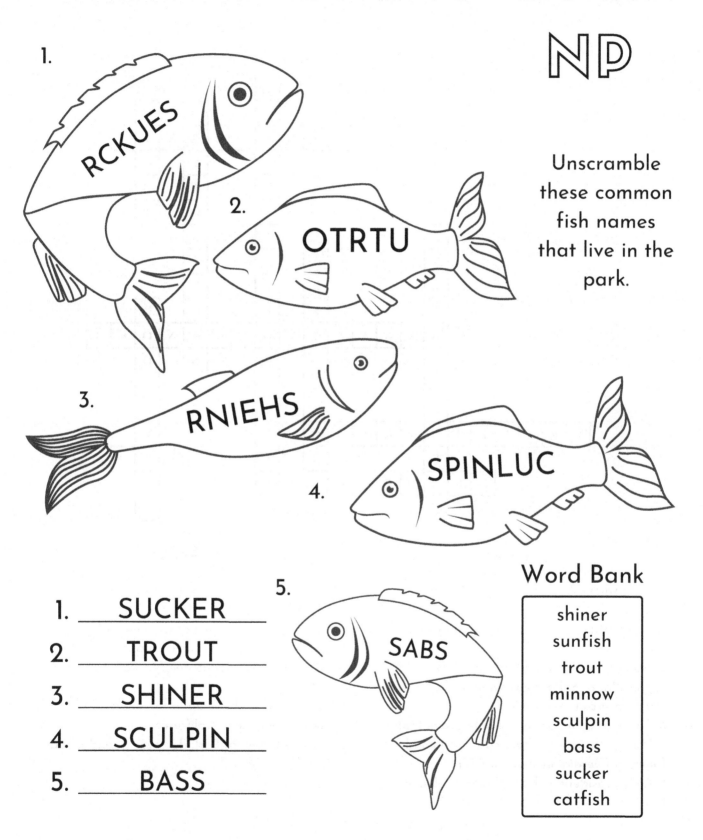

Unscramble these common fish names that live in the park.

1. RCKUES
2. OTRTU
3. RNIEHS
4. SPINLUC
5. SABS

1. __SUCKER__
2. __TROUT__
3. __SHINER__
4. __SCULPIN__
5. __BASS__

Word Bank

shiner
sunfish
trout
minnow
sculpin
bass
sucker
catfish

Answers: Other National Parks

Down

1. State where Acadia National Park is located
2. This National Park has the Spanish word for turtle in it
3. Number of National Parks in Alaska
5. This National Park has some of the hottest temperatures in the world
6. This National Park is the only one in Idaho
7. This toothsome creature can be famously found in Everglades National Park
8. Only president with a national park named for them

Across

4. This state has the most National Parks
9. This park has some of the newest land in the US, caused by a volcanic eruption
10. This park has the deepest lake in the United States
11. This color shows up in the name of a National Park in California
12. This National Park deserves a gold medal

Answers: Where National Park Will You Go Next?

1. Zion
2. Big Bend
3. Glacier
4. Olympic
5. Sequoia
6. Bryce
7. Mesa Verde
8. Biscayne
9. Wind Cave
10. Great Basin
11. Katmai
12. Yellowstone
13. Voyageurs
14. Arches
15. Badlands
16. Denali
17. Glacier Bay
18. Hot Springs

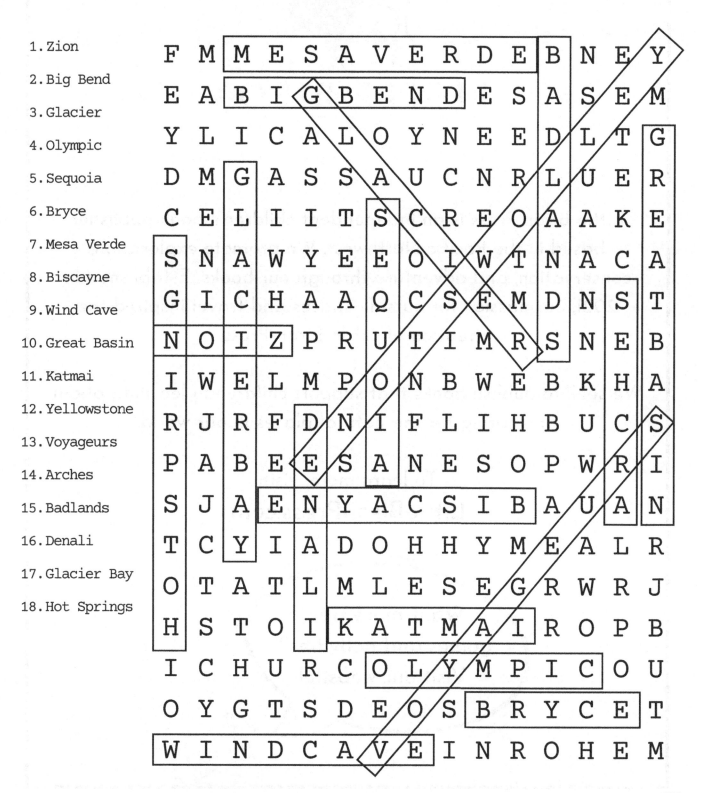

Little Bison Press is an independent children's book publisher based in the Pacific Northwest. We promote exploration, conservation, and adventure through our books. Established in 2021, our passion for outside spaces and travel inspired the creation of Little Bison Press.

We seek to publish books that support children in learning about and caring for the natural places in our world.

To learn more, visit:
LittleBisonPress.com

Made in United States
North Haven, CT
21 February 2024

49006125R00043